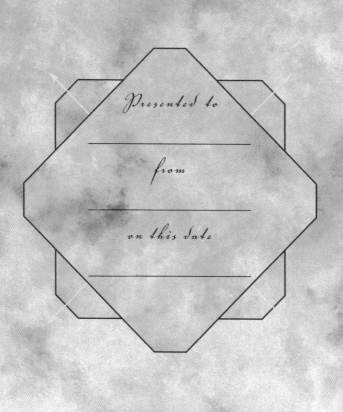

Presented to

_____

from

_____

on this date

_____

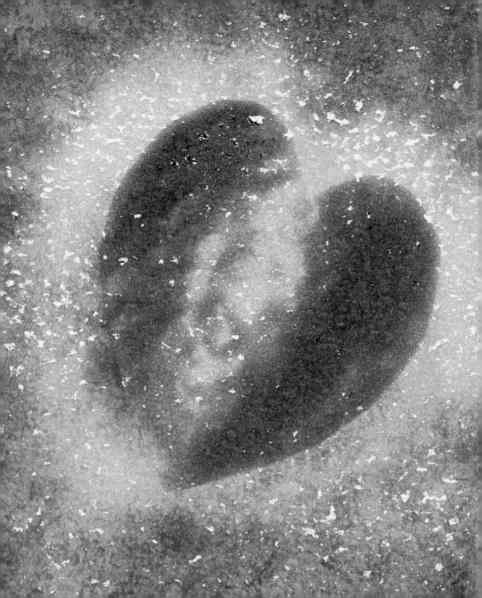

love

The greatest thing in the world

A DayMaker Greeting Book

faith

Hope Love

*S*INCE TIME BEGAN many people have believed that the greatest of all virtues in the spiritual realm is faith. The apostle Paul taught that if you may have enough faith to move a mountain, yet do not have love, you are nothing. ❧ Peter encourages us to love one another deeply. ❧ And John put it this way, simply: "GOD IS LOVE."

The Secret of a Fulfilled Life

If I have faith so that I can move mountains and have not love, I am nothing." Paul's words pierce because we've all felt the sting of words without sincerity and eloquence without love.

Love is far greater than charity because you can have charity without love. Give a coin to a beggar, and ease your conscience—but if we truly loved them we would either do more or less.

Paul contrasts love with sacrifice. The would-be missionary will do well to remember that though you die a martyr, yet have not love, your death would be in vain!

You may struggle to learn another language, but when you reach your country of destination, love, the universal language, will pour forth unconsciously. In Africa I encountered men and women who remembered the only white man they had ever seen before David Livingstone; and as you traced his footsteps there, men's faces lit up as they spoke of the kind doctor who passed through there. They could not understand him, but they felt the love that beat in his heart.

Love is endowed with the power to rouse the hearts of men and women everywhere to lofty purposes. Take love into your vocation and your lifework will succeed. It's not worth doing if you take anything less. You may achieve every accomplishment, and yet miss love.

Paul portrays love as a life light. Watch a beam of light pass through a crystal prism and you see it emerge on the other side revealing its various colors: red, blue, yellow, violet, orange—the colors of the rainbow. Paul passes this thing called love through the magnificent prism of his inspired intellect, and it emerges revealing its characteristics.

The Nine Aspects of Love

Patience

love will wait

PATIENCE   The attitude of love is passive, love waits to begin—does not hurry; it is calm; it is ready to do its work when the call comes but meanwhile wearing the ornament of a meek and quiet spirit. Love suffers long, bears all things, believes all things, hopes all things, and therefore waits.

KINDNESS   Active love. Notice how much time Jesus spent simply doing kind things? Study His life and you will see that He spent a great portion of His time simply encouraging people, doing good deeds for people. God has put within our power the ability to bring encouragement to those around us.

"The greatest thing a man can do for his heavenly Father," someone once said, "is to be kind to some of His other children." I wonder why we are not all kinder than we are. How much the world needs it. How easily it is done. How quickly it responds.

Love rewards itself—there is no debtor in the world so honorable as love. Love never fails. Love is success; love is happiness; love is life. Robert Browning said it well: "Love is the energy of life."

GENEROSITY

Love does not envy. This is love which competes with others. Whenever you attempt a good work, you will find others doing the same kind of work and probably doing it better. Do not envy them. Envy is an ill feeling toward those who are in the same line as ourselves. Even doing "God's work" is little protection against harboring this most ungodly feeling. That most despicable of all the moods that cloud a Christian's soul assuredly waits for us on the threshold of every work unless we are fortified with this grace of magnanimity.

Love Is the Desire

Noblest of All

Rindness

love is kind

HUMILITY

Having learned all that, you will have to learn one thing more: to put a seal upon your lips and forget what you have done. After you have been kind, after love has done its work, go back into the shade and say nothing about it. Love revels not in itself. Love waives adoration. "Love is not puffed up."

COURTESY

This attribute here is love in relation to etiquette. The secret to love is being polite—love cannot behave otherwise. The most uncultured person, if he or she has love stored up in the heart, will not behave unseemly.

Thomas Carlyle said there was no truer gentleman in Europe than Robert Burns, the ploughman poet. It was because he loved everything—from the mouse to the daisy; all things great and small that God had made. And with this simple passport he could mingle freely with any society, and enter courts and palaces from his humble cottage. And that is the whole art and mystery of it. A gentleman will not do ungentle things. And the gentle soul, the considerate, sympathetic nature cannot do anything else.

UNSELFISHNESS   "Love seeks not her own." In many countries the average citizen is devoted, and rightly so, to his or her rights. But there come times when a person may exercise the even higher right of giving up his or her rights. Yet Paul does not summon us to give up our rights. Love strikes much deeper.

"Do you seek great things for yourself?" asked the prophet. "Seek them not." Why? Because there is no greatness in things. There is no lasting joy acquiring things. Unfortunately, half the world is in hot pursuit of the wrong scent. He that would be great among you, said Jesus, let him serve. It is more blessed to give than to receive.

Generosity

love gladly gives

EVEN TEMPER   "Love is not easily provoked." Some view a hot temper as a harmless vice. Others see it as a disposition or family failing—not a thing to be taken too seriously. Yet the Bible condemns it as one of the most destructive elements in human nature. A hot temper is a symptom of a disease which lies beneath; the occasional bubble surfaces and reveals a rottenness in men and women of "touchy" disposition. Who can measure the damage to society from a hot temper—for breaking up communities, destroying marriages, devastating homes. For sheer gratuitous misery-producing power, it stands alone. Jealousy, pride, cruelty, and self-righteousness—all are at the root of it. Jesus declared, "Unless man be born again, he simply cannot enter the kingdom of heaven." Those who want to go to heaven must take heaven with them. Heaven has no room for moody persons.

A lack of patience, or kindness, or generosity, or courtesy, are all instantaneously revealed in one flash of temper.

A hot temper must be done away with. Souls are made sweet not by taking something out, but by putting something in. When God's heart envelops our own, it sweetens, purifies, and transforms. This radical change rehabilitates the heart. Willpower does not change men and women. Jesus does. "Let that mind be in you which was also in Christ Jesus." Some of us have no time to lose. It is a matter of life or death.

INNOCENCE   This aspect can be easily dismissed. Innocence is a grace and its possessors wield the secret of great personal influence. Influencers are people who believe in you. In a critical atmosphere, inwardly you die; but in an atmosphere of acceptance, you flourish. It's a wonderful thing when in this often hostile world you encounter someone who acts this way.

Humility

love is its own reward

Love "thinks no evil," imputes no motive, looks on the bright side, puts the best construction on every action. What a state of mind! What a blessing to meet such a friend for a day!

If we seek to elevate others, we soon see that success is in proportion to the degree of faith we had in them. When you respect another, their self-respect begins to grow and each can realize their full potential.

SINCERITY "Love rejoices not in iniquity, but. . . in the truth." The quality here is sincerity. One who loves will love truth. These rejoice in truth—not in what they have been taught to believe, not in a church doctrine, but "in the truth." They search for only what is genuine with humble, open minds and cherish truth when they find it.

Sincerity is restraint which refuses to capitalize on the weaknesses of others—it finds no pleasure in exposing their faults, but "covers all things". It endeavors to see things as they are and rejoices to find them better than may have been suspected.

The issue is to have love molded into our character. That is our life work to focus on in this world: to learn love. Life is ripe with opportunities to learn love: everyone, every day, is given many. This world is not a playground; it's a classroom, and the eternal lesson is learning how to love better.

What makes a good athlete? Practice. If you don't exercise your body, you won't develop muscle; without spiritual training, you won't develop strength of character. Love is a rich, vigorous expression of character—God's nature in all its fullness.

What did Jesus do in the carpenter's shop? Practice. The Bible tells us that He learned obedience and increased in wisdom and in favor with God and man.

love is patient.

love is kind.

it is not proud.

love keeps no

record of wrongs.

love rejoices

in truth.

love protects.

love trusts.

love endures.

Courtesy

love is polite

Don't grumble about the suffering you have experienced or the difficult people you live or work with. Don't be puzzled when temptation increases, seemingly unaffected by prayer. God allows these things—they are opportunities to grow patient, humble, generous, unselfish, courteous, and kind. Don't resent the hand that is molding your character. Don't avoid difficulties or obstacles. Don't isolate yourself. Mingle. Character is forged in the crucible of life—that is where we to learn love.

Love is more than the heart that beats within. We may try to emulate those who outwardly show it. But this will not bring love into our nature. The result comes as we love: We love Him—and we are compelled to love all people.

Look into the mirror and reflect the character of Jesus— and you will be changed into the same image, from tenderness to tenderness. Look to the Cross of Calvary, and you must love God.

Loving Jesus, you become like Him and become an attractive force, drawing all people to you. Like Him you will be drawn to all people. It's inevitable.

Edward Irving once visited a dying boy, and when he entered the room he just put his hand on the boy's head, and said, "My boy, God loves you," and went away. The boy called out from his bed and to the others in the house, "God loves me! God loves me!" It changed that boy. The sense of God's love overwhelmed him and created a new heart within him. God's love melts hearts and begins a new work in those who are patient, humble, gentle, and unselfish. There is no other way to get it. Love your friends; love your enemies; love everyone—because He first loved us.

Love Con

guers All

Unselfishness

love shares

Paul says, "Whether there be knowledge, it shall vanish away."
The wisdom of the ancients, where is it today? Great inventions
come and go. Paul focused on the wonders of his time, things
people prized most, and brushed them aside. He did not con-
demn these things in themselves yet emphasized that they would
not last. There are appealing things in the world; but they will
not endure. Love people rather than things.

Seek the abundant life; seek God's love. Seek God, for God is
love. Then love can take hold of you—body, soul, and spirit. Give
and it will be given back to you. Love is its own reward.

To love abundantly is to live abundantly. To love forever is
to live forever. Eternal life and love are intertwined. We rise each
day for the same reason: We want to live forever. Because there
are people who love you, and whom you want to see tomorrow,

and be with, and love. There's no greater reason for living than to love and to be loved. Because to live is to love. And eternal life is to know God; for God is love. That's the definition Jesus gave. Think about it.

If love is eternal, then in the final analysis, love is life. Love never fails, and life will never fail as long as there is love. No worse fate can befall a person than to live and grow old alone, neither loving nor being loved.

Love is patient and kind; it does not envy; it is not proud. Live this way and everything you do will be worth doing. Living them out, however, will require prayer and meditation, just as advancement requires preparation and diligence. Reflect on your life and you'll find that the times that stand out are the ones in which you have done things out of a spirit of love.

Even-tempered

love is not moody

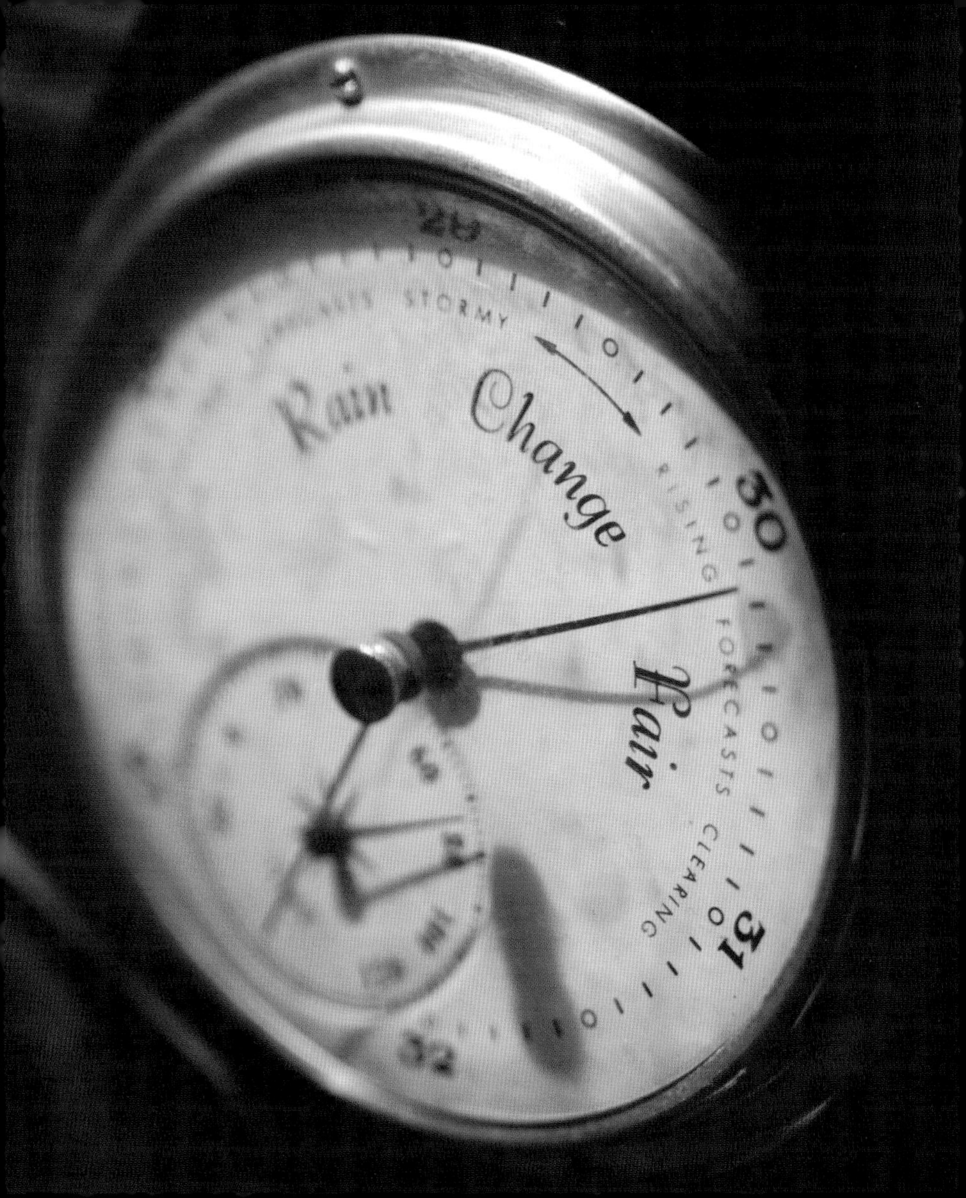

Rain
Change
Fair
STORMY
RISING
FORECASTS CLEARING
30
31

In the Book of Matthew, Judgment Day is depicted: God is sitting on His throne, dividing the sheep from the goats. The test then won't be what we have believed, nor what we have achieved, but how we have acted. In that indictment, sins of commission are not even referred to. By what we have not done, by sins of omission, we will be judged. For by withholding love we negate the love of Christ—proof that we never really knew Him. That He inspired nothing in our lives, that we were not moved by His compassion for the world, to love.

> "I LIVED FOR MYSELF, I THOUGHT FOR MYSELF,
>
> FOR MYSELF, AND NONE BESIDE—
>
> JUST AS IF JESUS HAD NEVER LIVED,
>
> AS IF HE HAD NEVER DIED."

Where love is, God is. God is love. Therefore love—without distinction, without calculation, without delay. Lavish it on the poor, the rich who often need it most—and on friends and family. Any act of kindness that you can show, do it now. Don't postpone it or neglect it, for you will not pass this way again.

A day is coming when God will gather all the nations of the world, the spectacle itself, the mere sight of it, will silently judge each one of them. Then we will meet either those we have met and helped, or the unpitied masses we have neglected. No charge will be brought, except lovelessness. Don't be fooled. The words that each of us hear that day will speak not of churches, but of life; not of saints, but of the hungry and the poor and the hurting; and compassion in the name of Jesus, who said: Whoever receives a little child in My name receives Me. FOR THIS REASON LIVE. FOR THIS REASON LOVE.

Innocence

love is blameless

JESUS SAID:

WHOEVER RECEIVES

A LITTLE CHILD

IN MY NAME

RECEIVES ME.

God

Is Love

Sincerity

love says, "I care"

Love is

the greatest

gift of all.

ISBN 1-58660-701-4

Cover images ©John Morrison/Photonica
Photo credits: page 41 ©Jane Yeomans; page 48 Brooke Fasani; page 50 Doug Plummer
Book design by Kevin Keller | designconcepts

Published by Barbour Books, an imprint of Barbour Publishing, Inc.,
P.O. Box 719, Uhrichsville, Ohio 44683, www.barbourbooks.com

Printed in China.
5 4 3 2 1